Joseph Breault

SEEKING PURITY OF HEART

The Gift of Ourselves to God

Introduction by George A. Maloney, S.J.

LIVING FLAME PRESS
BOX 74 LOCUST VALLEY, N.Y. 11560

All quotations of scripture are from the *Jerusalem Bible* copyright ©
1966 by Darton, Longman and Todd, Ltd., and Doubleday & Co.,
Inc., and are used by permission of the publisher.

The quotation by W.H. Auden on page 13 is from *For the Time
Being,* Faber and Faber, London, 1945, p. 124.

Nihil Obstat: Rev. Carl D. Hinrichsen
Imprimatur: Most Rev. Peter L. Gerety, March 6, 1975

Illustrations by Jacqueline Seitz
Cover by Robert Manning and Jacqueline Seitz

Published by:
Living Flame Press / Box 74 / Locust Valley / New York 11560

Copyright, 1975 Joseph Breault
ISBN: 0-914544-07-1

Contents

Introduction 5
Foreword 11
1 Sin Within Our Hearts 15
2 Scripture 19
3 The Desert Fathers 27
4 St. Bernard 35
5 The Twentieth Century 51
6 Giving Our Hearts to God 67
7 Conclusion 87
Notes 92

Introduction

God is again calling His people into the desert. And there He wishes to reveal Himself in a powerful, unifying way beyond words and images, in the immediacy of a Lover to His beloved.

Like Moses in the desert, tending Jethro's flocks, this people is hearing God's command to strip themselves of every control they have over their lives. Moses heard God's command to take off his shoes. When he did, a new revelation of God came over him. God revealed Himself to Moses as a burning, devouring fire. His first impulse was one of curiosity. He wanted to go forward by his own powers in order to comprehend the exterior "why" of God through his reasoning powers. But he learned that the first step to receive God's intimate revelation of Himself was to be stripped, unencumbered by his own self. Moses became God's prophet when he was completely purified in his heart having taken off his shoes, leaving behind all of his securities and protections.

God is not a land to be conquered by man's force. He is a Holy Land toward which man approaches with bare feet, a symbol of total emptiness of his own power, of purity of heart.

Carl Jung pointed out that the impoverished West had lost the ability to commune with the Absolute through myths and symbols, archetypal models implanted in man's unconscious. The scientific Western world has been rich in techniques but poor in intuitions, in the "feminine" receptivity to the inner voice of God who resides in the "temple invisible."

The rise in anxieties and stresses in our lives along with our mounting inability to cope with the speed and meaninglessness of our lives is causing us great mental illnesses. We desperately need to communicate with God on a more total level of consciousness.

But the first step to our receiving a deeper revelation of God is always that of the Gospel — a call to conversion, to a *metanoia*. In Greek this word connotes a complete turning of man back to God. His heart, the core of his being that gave ultimate direction to his life, had to be purified.

Jesus Christ preached this total turning to God when He repeated the great Shema: "Thou shalt love the Lord thy God with thy whole heart. . . . "

He promised His disciples: "Blessed are the pure of heart for they shall see God."

When the Christians in the fourth century no longer reached such purity of heart by bodily martyrdom, many "athletes" of Christ went out literally into the desert and there day and night begged Jesus the Divine Physician to heal their conscious and unconscious levels and thus raise them to a new cosmic superconsciousness of transfigured sons of God, already participating in the resurrection of Jesus Christ.

Today many Christians are tired of living double lives, part-time as Christ-centered humans and part-time as this-world-centered citizens. They desire to move beyond a surface Christianity and invite Jesus to become Lord and Master over even their unconscious. They seriously take St. Paul's advice: "Be not conformed to this world, but be transformed by the renewal of your mind" (Rom. 12:2). They are tired of living their Christianity in such a superficial way that when the thin veneer is scratched a whole area of interior darkness, selfishness, prejudice, resentment is exposed as unhealed.

The best way to clean the surface of a lake is not by skimming the top but by purifying the source of the flow from the wellsprings at the bottom. In all of us there are hidden recesses in our unconscious that the healing power of Jesus Christ has not yet touched.

Purity of heart is an attitude of the Christian, of constant conversion, of turning to the indwelling Trinity abiding within him and crying out constantly that every past memory, every experience of yesterday, last year or at the beginning of consciousness, be brought under Jesus Christ. "Cast down the imaginations and bring into captivity every thought to the obedience of Christ" *(2 Cor. 10:5).*

We are the total of all experiences we have allowed to enter through our senses, imagination, intellect and will into our storeroom of our unconscious. But we who "have been predestined to be conformed to the image of His Son" *(Rom. 8:28)* are even more when all of our past experiences are brought into a healed synthesis by the power of Christ's Spirit of love. "That He would grant you, according to the riches of His glory to be strengthened with might by His Spirit in the inner man, that Christ may dwell in your hearts by faith" *(Eph. 3:16).*

The purifying of our hearts by the indwelling of the Holy Spirit is the topic of this present work by Joe Breault. It is a most important topic as old as the Old and New Testament, as freshly new as the latest teaching on psycho-cybernetics. Purity of heart is what happens to man in his consciousness and unconscious levels of being when by God's purifying love man enters into a new state of integration, the new creation that St. Paul speaks of: "And for anyone who is in Christ, there is a new creation; the old creation has gone, and now the new one is here" *(2 Cor. 5:17).* Purity of heart is nothing more than the fulfillment of the evangelical plan of Christ, that is, the restoration of the

Divine Image. In true, authentic Christian prayer, cultural differences seem to disappear and a common experience talks to all human beings who have had the courage and tenacity to enter into the "desert" of their heart and there do battle.

The author has assembled solid teaching on purity of heart as gathered from Holy Scripture, the Desert Fathers, St. Bernard, and the twentieth century sources such as Vatican II and Father Bernard Lonergan, S.J. He shows in a concrete way how we are to let go and give our hearts to God, in relations to others in a community and in one-to-one personal relationships, to ourselves and to God.

William James described man's consciousness as "the red-hot point of consciousness." In all of us there is a center of the cyclone, to use the title of John C. Lilly's book. For those who have the courage and persistence to enter and touch that center of the cyclone, God's grace moves them with a warming of their hearts and makes their whole being glad with an ineffable, inflaming love for God and man, enlightening the mind and pouring out into their interior feelings of great joy. Man becomes, under the power of the Holy Spirit, a "whole" person, body, soul, spirit, his conscious and unconscious levels totally under the healing power of God's love. Such a Christian knows that he has broken on to a new level of understanding himself in relation to God and to the rest of the world around him. The words of Jesus Christ become a reality daily as man truly sees God every-

Foreword

This is a story of the journey towards purity of heart. Jesus, the Way, the Truth, and the Life, has called us to have hearts wherein he dwells, to give ourselves to God.

We follow Jesus, the Way, as Guide on our journey to become what we are called to be. On the way we meet monsters within our hearts, and have many adventures as we trust in his power whereby we gain an ever fuller victory.

We seek Jesus, the Truth, even in the midst of anxiety within and without. As we journey towards the freedom of the children of God, he gives us brothers and sisters to support us. In a mysterious way we come home to the brethren, as we grow in the interior freedom that is purity of heart.

We fall in love with Jesus, the Life, even as we wade through the swamp of our impurity, rebellion, illusions and desire to be someone other than we are. As we taste his life, and our hearts unite with his to be one flesh, we rejoice in freedom, fullness, peace and love.

We can take Mary as an example. When told that Jesus would be conceived in her womb, she could not understand, yet trusted in the power of God and the promised Holy Spirit: " 'I am the handmaid of the Lord,' said Mary 'let what you have said be done to me' " *(Luke 1:38).* What happened in Mary's womb, God has both promised and decreed, is to happen in our hearts. Jesus is to be born in hearts which are pure, filled with love, and which have banished everything that ties down or binds them.

I write this while on retreat at Our Lady of the Holy Cross Abbey, whose monks I wish to thank for their generosity toward me. They have taught me about the journey as they shared their life. The name of the Abbey is so significant — Our Lady of the Holy Cross. It brings to mind that those who are to have Christ born in them must be of the Holy Cross. As we walk the journey in faith, God strips us of everything but himself.

Those from whom I learn the most about the journey are the brothers and sisters I live with in Ignatius House Community, Rutherford, New Jersey. As we journey, we become aware that we travel together, supporting one another in the Body of Christ. I am grateful to all my brethren who have been for me a source of the life of Jesus.

I pray that what is shared about the journey will be an encouragement for each of us to travel courageously from sin within our hearts to an ever-growing purity of heart and freedom, which is our birthright as children of God. Lastly, a few poetic lines from W.H. Auden's *For the Time Being* that speak crisply and incisively about the journey:

> *He is the Way.*
> *Follow Him through the Land of Unlikeness;*
> *You will see rare beasts, and have unique adventures.*

> *He is the Truth.*
> *Seek Him in the Kingdom of Anxiety;*
> *You will come to a great city that has expected your return for years.*

> *He is the Life.*
> *Love Him in the World of the Flesh;*
> *And at your marriage all its occasions shall dance for joy.*

January 23, 1975
Berryville, Virginia

13

Sin within our hearts.

1

Sin Within Our Hearts

There is a passage in the ninth chapter of John's gospel that many Christians find distressing. It appears after Jesus cures the man born blind and the Pharisees question the latter repeatedly, finally driving him away. The passage is:

"Jesus said: 'It is for judgment that I have come into this world, so that those without sight may see and those with sight turn blind.' Hearing this, some Pharisees who were present said to him, 'We are not blind, surely?' Jesus replied: 'Blind? If you were, you would not be guilty, but since you say, "We see," your guilt remains.' " *(John 9:39-41)*

The meaning we draw from this passage is that the complacent who see by their own light will

15

turn "blind" as a result of Jesus' coming into the world.[1] The Pharisees protest that *they* see and therefore are not blind. Jesus agrees that they *do* see, but by their own light, and therefore they are guilty. The Pharisees did not want to understand deeply enough, they were only concerned with self-righteous seeing and not with the source of their sight.

What is so distressing in this passage is the question it raises about the source of our own sight. "Blind Pharisee! Clean the inside of cup and dish first so that the outside may become clean as well" *(Matthew 23:26).* We wonder if the words of Jesus do not apply to us. We are disturbed at the thought that there is impurity inside of us, that there is sin deep within our hearts.

An experience I had one day helped me to see the depth of sin within my own heart. I had been praying in a chapel and while I was kneeling, I began to daydream, to slouch and fall half asleep. Suddenly I heard a noise outside and the doors opened. I quickly knelt upright and tried to pray again. I was very concerned to appear to be in prayer to whomever was entering. The experience made me wonder how clean the inside of my cup and dish were. Was I trying to serve God or to please men? Was my focus on Jesus or on appearing "religious" to people? I felt distressed.

I began to see and to accept the present limitations of my heart. This insight pierced an illusion I had about myself, that of my sanctity. It revealed to me my true self. The distress I felt was a grace, a work of the Holy Spirit, for at the same time I experienced freedom. I felt liberated from that kind of self-deception. It no longer had the same power over me. I was grateful to have seen how dark was my blindness. There was something inside me that God wanted to transform by the power of his love, and the compunction I felt, though quiet, was powerful. It was changing me. The Holy Spirit was purifying my heart, Jesus was present there.

What a gift to see the darkness! It is an opportunity for those of us without sight to see, to be grieved that we are blind. Jesus can then remove our guilt and give us his own light as we resolve to be responsive to the deep spiritual truth he has opened to our sight. What a delightful affliction to give ourselves over to the light of Jesus that reveals the darkness of our hearts! What joy we experience as we consider what we have been saved from: "If then, the light inside you is darkness, what darkness that will be!" *(Matthew 6:23)*. There is even greater joy in considering what we have been saved for: "Happy the pure in heart: they shall see God" *(Matthew 5:8)*. And all of this by the power of his love!

Who has the right to climb the mountain of Yahweh . . . he whose heart is pure.

2

Scripture

The words of Jesus: "Happy the pure in heart: they shall see God" *(Matthew 5:8)*, are a culmination of a long scriptural tradition. The Old Testament concept of purity is a negative and passive state meaning freedom from contamination by any sort of impurity, whether it be legal or physical. Most impurities, if they did not disappear of their own accord, after a period of time were removed by a washing or sacrifice.

Impurity in the Old Testament was seen as a defilement incompatible with God's purity and holiness, but purity conferred fitness to approach the sanctuary where Yahweh meets his people:

"Who has the right to climb the mountain of Yahweh, who the right to stand in his holy place? He whose hands are clean, whose heart is pure . . . " *(Psalm 24:3-4)*

Approaching the sanctuary was metaphorically called "seeing God" or "seeking his face" and means nothing more than to stand in his presence like servants before a kindly master.[2]

Yet the Hebrews would always recall God's reply to Moses when he asked to see the glory, the visible reality, of God:

"Moses said, 'Show me your glory, I beg you.' And he said, 'I will let all my splendour pass in front of you, and I will pronounce before you the name Yahweh . . . you cannot see my face,' he said 'for man cannot see me and live.' " *(Exodus 33:18-20)*

God's sanctity is so removed from man's unworthiness that man must perish if he looks on God. God is holy. To see the face of God is to die because man's impurity cannot live in the presence of God's holiness. This tenet was expressed in the concept of ritual impurity. An example is the regulation from *Leviticus* concerning the purification of a woman after childbirth:

"If a woman conceives and gives birth to a boy, she is to be unclean for seven days, just as she is unclean during her monthly periods. On the eighth day the child's foreskin must be circumcised, and she must wait another thirty-three days for her blood to be purified. She must not touch anything consecrated nor go to the sanctuary until the time of her purification is over . . . she is to bring to the priest at the entrance to the Tent of Meeting a lamb one year old for a holocaust, and a young pigeon or turtledove as a sacrifice for sin. The priest is to offer this before Yahweh, perform the rite of atonement over her, and she will be purified from her flow of blood . . . If she cannot afford a lamb, she is to take two turtledoves or two young pigeons, one for the holocaust and the other for the sacrifice for sin." *(Leviticus 12:2-4, 6-8)*

The woman's ritual purity was considered to be lost by childbirth and re-established by the above rites. Mary, the mother of Jesus, submitted herself to this law, giving the offering of the poor *(Luke 2:22f)*.

By the time the book of Job was written, the uncleanness of man was recognized as going far deeper than ritual impurity: "How can any man be clean? Born of woman, can he ever be good?" *(Job 15:14)*. There is something far deeper that makes man unholy, incapable of standing in the presence of God. Man was created in God's image and likeness, yet something, which the beginning of Genesis illustrates, happened that has made man intrinsically unclean.

To see God, to enter into God's presence, one must be purified. Isaiah recounts seeing God in a vision:

" . . . I saw the Lord Yahweh seated on a high throne; his train filled the sanctuary; above him stood seraphs . . . And they cried out one to another in this way, 'Holy, holy, holy is Yahweh

Sabaoth. His glory fills the whole earth.' The foundations of the threshold shook with the voice of the one who cried out, and the Temple was filled with smoke. I said: 'What a wretched state I am in! I am lost, for I am a man of unclean lips and I live among a people of unclean lips, and my eyes have looked at the King, Yahweh Sabaoth.' Then one of the seraphs flew to me, holding in his hand a live coal which he had taken from the altar with a pair of tongs. With this he touched my mouth and said: 'See now, this has touched your lips, your sin is taken away, your iniquity is purged.' " *(Isaiah 6:1-7)*

To see God one must be purified by a burning fire, for God is a consuming fire *(Deuteronomy 4:24; Hebrews 12:29).*

The prophets' mission entailed a call to a deeper notion of purity. They constantly proclaimed that neither ablutions nor sacrifices have any value in and of themselves, but only as a sign of interior purification. Jeremiah proclaims: "Wash your heart clean of wickedness, Jerusalem, and so be saved" *(Jeremiah 4:14).* No longer your clothes or body, but your heart.

The meanings of the word "heart" are very different in Hebrew and English, except for the physiological sense as a central organ of the body. What we mean by "heart" is the center of our emotions or affective life. It is common to hear a person say, "I love you with all my heart." If a Hebrew wanted to say that, he might use these words: "I love you with all my kidneys." The Old Testament uses the word "heart" to indicate a wider range of meaning than emotions. It means *all* that is within a man, not only his emotions, but also his will, memory, thinking, planning, and reasoning powers. For example, one's understanding is in the heart, whereas we might say "the head" *(Deuteronomy 29:4 — "*... Yahweh has given you no heart to understand ... "). One's decision to carry out what God orders is made in the heart, whereas we would say the will *(I Samuel 13:14 —* "Yahweh has searched out a man for himself after his own heart and designated him leader of his people, since you have not carried out what Yahweh ordered you"). Even one's thoughts are in the heart, whereas we would say "the mind" *(Daniel 2:30 —* the literal translation is: "the thoughts of your heart," Jerusalem Bible translates as "inmost thoughts," New American Bible translates as "the thoughts of your own mind").[3] The heart of man, then, is his whole conscious, intelligent and free personality. It signifies the inner life as opposed to the outer actions which spring from it.

When the prophets proclaim: "Purify your hearts!" the concept of purity has a new interiority. No longer wash your clothes, but your heart, your whole inner self. Purity of heart is a metaphor for the removal of inner defilement, the very source of sin within us, our inner disposition. What is beginning to be cleansed is that deep impurity which is man's pride. This involves even our thoughts, as Jeremiah continues:

"Wash your heart clean of wickedness, Jerusalem, and so be saved. How long will you harbour in your breast your pernicious thoughts?" *(Jeremiah 4:14)*

In Hebrew, to think means to devise, to conceive, to bring something into being in the heart. The thoughts of our hearts need to be purified. Jesus goes even further than the prophets in his emphasis on inner purity:

"He called the people to him and said, 'Listen and understand. What goes into the mouth does not make a man unclean; it is what comes out of the mouth that makes him unclean ... the things that come out of the mouth come from the heart, and it is these that make a man unclean. For from the heart come evil intentions: murder, adultery, fornication, theft, perjury, slander. These are the things that make a man unclean. But to eat with unwashed hands does not make a man unclean.' " *(Matthew 15:10-11, 18-20)*

The Old and New Testaments agree that the true sources of impurity, which separate man from God, are the evil inclinations of the thoughts of the heart. Man is powerless, he cannot cleanse his own heart, he cannot save himself. Only God can save him. The Psalmist cries out: "God, create a clean heart in me, put into me a new and constant spirit" *(Psalm 51:10)*. And God promises to save him: "I will give them a heart to acknowledge that I am Yahweh" *(Jeremiah 24:7)*. God promises a new heart and a new spirit:

"I shall give you a new heart, and put a new spirit in you; I shall remove the heart of stone from your bodies and give you a heart of flesh instead. I shall put my spirit in you." *(Ezekiel 36:26-27)*

God's method for reversing the evil inclinations of our hearts is to strengthen man by his own Holy Spirit. Ritual purifications in the early Old Testament involved washings and sacrifice. Purification of our hearts involves the washing of baptism, the pouring out of the Holy Spirit into our hearts, the sacrifice of Jesus on the cross, and our faith in him, for St. Luke writes: "God . . . purified their hearts by faith" *(Acts 15:9)*. Jesus' word is that he has come to baptize with the Holy Spirit and with fire. This is charged with meaning in the whole prophetic tradition of purity of heart. Jesus has come to baptize in the Holy Spirit and to purify our hearts, our whole inner self, that we might see the face of the living God. No longer is this to be a figure of speech, but a spiritual reality! And it is in Jesus that it is easier for heaven and earth to pass away than for one who has sought God not to find him. St. John writes of the culmination of all history, when "The throne of God and the Lamb will be in its place in the city; his servants will worship him, they will see him face to face" *(Revelation 22:3-4)*.

Focus your gaze on the immediate goal, purity of heart.

3

The Desert Fathers

In the preceding scriptural passages, we saw the centrality of purity of heart within the biblical tradition, its link with the coming of the Holy Spirit into the hearts of men and with the vision of God, and above all, the relationship of purity of heart to freedom from evil thoughts.

Both the term and the concept, "purity of heart," are found frequently in the earliest Christian writings. It is here that we can see more clearly what purity of heart means in our everyday life and thoughts. The following sayings from the Desert Fathers of the fourth century make it clear that purity of heart is not synonymous with the absence of evil thoughts.

"One of the elders said: it is not because evil

thoughts come to us that we are condemned, but only because we make use of the evil thoughts. It can happen that from these thoughts we suffer shipwreck, but it can also happen that because of them we may be crowned.[4]

"A brother came to Abbot Pastor and said: 'Many distracting thoughts come into my mind, and I am in danger because of them.' Then the elder thrust him out into the open air and said: 'Open up the garments about your chest and catch the wind in them.' But he replied: 'This I cannot do.' So the elder said to him: 'If you cannot catch the wind, neither can you prevent distracting thoughts from coming into your head. Your job is to say no to them.' "[5]

Purity of heart, then, does not mean that a person no longer experiences any evil or distracting thoughts; rather, the person does not yield or consent to them. This is called guarding one's thoughts or custody of the heart. In fact, what these passages are saying is that not yielding to evil thoughts is a source of growth. It is useless to be anxious about the evil and distractions coming our way, for we can no more avoid them than we could catch the wind in our coats.

The Desert Fathers did a great deal of fasting and practiced physical austerities which might imply to some that the body is evil. It is important to realize that evil thoughts and impurities are not caused by the existence of a body. In Hebrew thought there is no division between body and soul as there is in Greek. For Jesus, the source of impurity and evil is not the body and its urges, rather it is the heart and its evil thoughts.

"For it is from within, from men's hearts, that evil intentions emerge: fornication, theft, murder, adultery, avarice, malice, deceit, indecency, envy, slander, pride, folly. All these evil things come from within and make a man unclean." *(Mark 7:21-23)*

Jesus is concerned here with deliberate intentions, not with the feelings or vague thoughts that arise from sources that are only recently beginning to be fathomed by psychology. Confusion here may cause some persons to think that all their inner desires and hostilities should be repressed, rather than freely examined so as to determine their message and make a moral judgment.[6]

A further insight lies within the distinction between the power of sin over us and the existence of sin within us. St. Paul writes in Romans that we must not let sin reign in our mortal bodies *(Romans 6:12)*, and that sin will no longer dominate our lives since we are living by grace *(Romans 6:14)*. He does not say that the existence of sin within our hearts will die while we are still in this world, but rather that its power over us will cease.[7] Purity of heart does not mean that evil thoughts are unknown, rather, they are not yielded to and thus have no power over us.

Another story of the Desert Fathers is related by Cassian.[8] He tells how one day he went into the Egyptian desert to seek out Abbot Moses, a famous hermit. Upon finding him, Cassian begged him for some words of wisdom, and reluctantly Abbot Moses presented this question to him:

"All the arts and sciences have some immediate goal or mark of their own for which the artist or scientist endures all hardships if only he can achieve that goal. Consider a farmer. A farmer endures the heat of the sun, the frost, the

cold and the tiredness of his body, yet he is always ploughing and caring for the field, keeping his goal in mind — that by hard work he can have a good field which is free from weeds and soft enough for plants to grow. In this way he can achieve his ultimate end which is to secure a large crop from which he can live free from care and increase his possessions.

"Our profession also has an immediate goal or mark for which we endure all sorts of hardships, not merely without weariness, but actually with delight — hunger from fasting, tiredness from vigils, body aches from sleeping on the hard ground, constant reading and meditation upon the scriptures, as well as the horrors of the desert which do not terrify us. You also endure many similar things. Answer me this: what is the goal or mark which incites you to endure all these things so cheerfully?"

Cassian replied: "We endure all this for the sake of the kingdom of God." Abbot Moses said: "Well spoken of the ultimate end, but what is the immediate goal or mark which, if we focus on it, will gain our ultimate end?" Cassian frankly confessed his ignorance.

Abbot Moses continued: "The first thing in all arts and sciences is to have some immediate goal, for man needs a focus for the mind and a constant mental purpose. Unless a man keep this before him with persistance, he will never achieve his ultimate end which he wants. For as I said before, the farmer has the ultimate end of living free from care with plenty; but the focus of his mind is a more immediate goal, namely, to have a good field clear from all weeds. The farmer knows that there is no other way to insure wealth, except the road that leads to it.

31

"The ultimate end of our way of life is indeed the kingdom of God. Yet you need to know the immediate goal, otherwise you will wear yourself out to no purpose. The immediate aim or goal is purity of heart, without which no one can gain the kingdom of God which is the ultimate end. Focus your energy and gaze then on purity of heart, as on a definite mark. If your thoughts wander from it, bring back your gaze to it.

"Perfection does not come from giving things up, but only in that love which consists in purity of heart alone. For 'not to be envious,' 'not to be puffed up,' 'not to be angry,' 'not to seek one's own advantage,' 'not to rejoice in another's sins,' 'not to think and consent to evil,' what is all this except ever to offer to God a perfect and clean heart, and to keep it free from all disturbances?

"It is for the sake of this purity of heart that we must do all that we do and seek all that we seek. For the sake of purity of heart we seek solitude, fastings, vigils, labor, poor clothing, reading and all the rest. Through these practices we hope to be able to keep our hearts untouched by the assaults of all the passions, and by these steps we hope to ascend to perfect love."

The story that Cassian relates urges us to seek actively purity of heart as the way to the kingdom of God. The early Fathers make clear that asceticism is merely a preliminary. It is faith which purifies the heart *(Acts 15:9)*, faith in Jesus and in the Holy Spirit who has been given to us. Purity of heart is the end result of yielding to the love of God and being made into a new creation. It is synonymous with our attachment to God in love, with the complete offering of ourselves to God, with agape.[9] It is seeking to serve and rejoice the heart of Jesus, not for rewards but simply to please him, with whom we are in love.

After the fall, man retained the image of God but lost his likeness.

state of man: man was made in the image and likeness of God. After the fall, however, man retained
the image of God but lost the likeness. The image
of God is understood to be our free-will, our capacity to consent. This cannot be lost since it is the
very essence of our humanity. Likeness to God
includes a life of agape-love, a freedom from self-
preoccupation, self-centeredness, and all the various ways in which we rationalize and distort reality
to have us look well even to ourselves. This likeness
to God can be, and has been, lost. Yet it can be
restored through grace, through the death and
resurrection of Jesus, through the outpouring of
the Holy Spirit.

What does this land of unlikeness look like? All
men have retained the image of God, the basic freedom to consent, yet most have not regained the
likeness to God which is the life of charity; it is
this we want to investigate: what is the person like
who has not regained the likeness to God?

Fundamentally, unlikeness means being centered
on ourselves and therefore plunged into unreality
since we are not centered on the source of all reality. However, reality still exists and we are still the
image of our Creator. Not possessing the life of
agape, in a sense, we are unreal, dead, a distortion
and caricature of our true selves which is in opposition to the love and will of God.

The basic defilement of fallen man is his profound, yet illusory, conviction that the universe is
centered upon himself in a way that it can only be
centered upon the living God. We attempt to

impose ourselves in every situation as distinct and superior beings, desiring to control everyone and everything. We turn all love inward and desire only that which we falsely perceive as our own personal good. We possess the semi-conscious conviction that we *deserve* to have our desires met. We have a ridiculous fixation on our own wills that paradoxically makes us slaves of them. We do not want to accept our own humanity and limitations. In short, we want to be omnipotent.

This spiritual pride, this refusal to submit to control, causes us to use all our "natural" psychological defense mechanisms [11] to create a false-self which satisfies our pride, an unreal world around ourselves, a facade which hides the truth from ourselves. We become more and more committed to deluding ourselves and making ourselves blind to our blindness. We become hard of heart.

Much of this may seem unfamiliar to us. Certainly, we say to ourselves, I do not want to be a god and omnipotent. Most of us are not foolish enough to think that we should be gods and far superior to every other being in the universe. We do want to be *relatively* omnipotent, though. We want the power to have what we want, the power to enjoy what we have, the power to demand that our wishes always be satisfied and our wills never frustrated or opposed, the power to be always right, the power to have other people need us and depend upon us. We want the fulfillment of our need to have everyone bow to our judgments, accepting our declarations as law. We want our unique answers to these questions are very important.

This twisting of reality, through focusing everything on ourselves, is what St. Paul writes of in the opening chapters of Romans. It is the cause of all our fear and despair, unhappiness and sorrow, anxiety and dissatisfaction, doubts, frustrations, conflicts, ambivalences, hesitations, insecurities, compulsive needs and attachments, isolation, loneliness, jealousy and envy, alienation and selfishness.

As we probe within to discover the unique manner in which our love is centered upon ourselves, we discover our particular fears and anxieties. And in the light of God's love we gradually are freed from them. This is no easy task and we need the power of the Spirit of Jesus to enlighten us, even to encourage us to want to know the truth.

I recall the time I was slouching in the chapel, and how I quickly knelt upright as the door opened. I reflected on what this revealed about the way in which I am focused upon myself. I had a fear of being regarded as less than perfect. I became aware of my desire to have others hold me in high esteem and of the anxiety that I experienced when I thought they did not. I encountered a conflict within my heart because, at the same time, I really did want to serve God alone, not caring about what other people thought. I hesitated to affirm that either one of these opposites was there since the other was. I saw the source of the insecurity in my life, my ambivalence over the fact that I wanted to serve God alone. As I prayed about this,

I felt more free than ever before from the need for public approval and from the fear, anxiety, hesitation and insecurity it involved.

The point is that most of our actions reveal a subtle desire for relative omnipotence of one kind or another. As silly and trivial as these may seem, our actions are a means of allowing God's light to reveal and cast out the darkness in our hearts. They are opportunities to become aware of our false-ego-self, to recognize its illusion and to be freed from it in a profound way.

On one hand, these things appear so ridiculous, on the other, they affect us so deeply. This subsurface desire for relative omnipotence makes it clear that there is a radical falsity within us that rots away our moral life in its very root because it makes all we do more or less a lie. This radical claim to relative omnipotence is the deep impurity of heart that stains and divides and enslaves our souls. This is what Jesus is talking about when he says to "repent and believe the good news." This is what he is saving us from. He is leading us on a journey out of the land of unlikeness.

This "land of unlikeness" that St. Bernard speaks of is inhabited by many types of people whom the gospel would call lukewarm, but who are socially acceptable in the world: a proud and tyrannical parent, a tearful and demanding martyr parent, a sadistic and overbearing boss, a nagging perfectionist, a self-righteous religious, a busybody and taleteller, a cynic and judge of everyone, a bossy and demanding friend, a misunderstood prophet, a self-pitying idealist, and a psuedo-saint (seeking sanctity and religious perfection as an unconscious satisfaction of this deep hidden impurity of heart which is man's pride and selfishness).

Asceticism as a Preliminary

The question we will explore further is this: How does one leave this land of unlikeness and enter deeply into God's love and mercy? The path St. Bernard proposes is based on the words of Jesus:

"... unless a wheat grain falls on the ground and dies, it remains only a single grain; but if it dies, it yields a rich harvest." *(John 12:24)*

"For anyone who wants to save his life will lose it; but anyone who loses his life for my sake will find it." *(Matthew 16:25)*

Bernard says the preliminary to the journey into purity of heart is asceticism. This may conjure up the wierdest thoughts, yet something quite simple is indicated. There do exist necessities of nature which have a priority *of time* over everything. They do not, however, have a priority *of importance*. The distinction between these two types of priorities is crucial. For instance, consider a husband who receives a call from his boss at night saying there is an emergency business situation that needs to be taken care of and he is to come at once. Assume this is rare, and that the husband does not really want to go, but realizes he has to. If his wife asks, "What's more important, me or your job?" the answer is that his wife is more important. She has the priority of importance. If the husband experiences a deep conflict, it means that the less important priority, the job, may have to be changed. However, in this situation the job has a priority of time (the husband goes in to take care of the emergency), and the priority of importance (loving his wife) does not mean that the job is to be ignored.

The same holds true for our relationship to God as opposed to the necessities of nature such as food, drink, shelter, clothing, etc. The love of God has the priority of importance, yet here and now, the necessities of nature have priority of time.

The problem arises when we place a priority of importance on the "necessities" of nature. When "useless pleasures" are sought for their own sake, apart from supporting us and God's life in us, things begin to go awry inside of us. The things we look to for satisfaction prove incapable of giving it, for we were not made for this. It is a false path and there is no freedom in following it. One is constantly wearying of what one has and is always hungering for new pleasure. The capacity for love within us is simply too great to be filled by anything other than God himself.

This is what St. Bernard means when he says that asceticism is a preliminary. It is a means and a check to insure that only the pleasure of God himself has a priority of importance.

The Three Steps of Truth

As the normal state of the body is health, so the normal state of the heart is purity. Asceticism is a preliminary, but it does not purify our hearts. Bernard writes of the journey as three steps of truth that lead to such purity of heart, the love which is God's Spirit.[12]

The first step is self-knowledge or humility: knowing and acknowledging our actual spiritual state, realizing that we are sinners (a lost likeness to God — not living in love) although we are the very image of God (a capacity to consent — free will). What it means to be a sinner, to have a lost likeness to God, is not merely a doctrinal belief that we have no feel for.

The incidences of the supper table and praying in the chapel illustrate the importance of being in touch with our sinfulness, the way we focus on ourselves, the lack of focus on serving and loving others, and the unique way in which we do that. These examples can offer practical help in attaining that self-knowledge, conscious that it always depends on the work of God's Spirit.

When you see a symptom work back to the "disease." The problem (what we need to repent of) is not really the actions we perform but the underlying attitudes and view of ourselves that motivates the actions. To put it concisely: real repentance is repenting of the "disease," not just the symptoms.

How do you work back to the "disease"? When

you see a wrong action, ask yourself, "Why?" Consider the example of slouching while praying in the chapel. The symptom is quickly kneeling upright because someone is coming. It is not sinful in itself, yet something is not quite right. As I reflected on it above (see page 39) and tried to work back to the "disease," certain things became clear. I was conscious of a fear and anxiety, a hesitation and insecurity. Why did I have such feelings? Was I really concerned about giving a good example and not scandalizing the person who would see me half-asleep rather than in prayer? Not at all. As I prayed, it was evident that I wanted people to respect and esteem me in a way that was not really proper. Certainly there is a healthy way in which people can respect you and there is nothing wrong in desiring that, yet I had a desire for esteem that was unhealthy. The particular sinful desire was that I be esteemed as only God should be: limitlessly and unquestioningly. I wanted people to view me according to my will, not in accord with reality. This is the subsurface "disease" that needs repentance. As I prayed, the Lord did give me a repentant heart and this grace of real repentance freed me in a deeper way from that desire.

When we see a symptom and work back to the disease, God will show us more and more what our root problems are, and heal them. The whole false-ego-self we have created will be frightened when this happens, it will refuse to see its pretentiousness, it will rebel against the emerging insight into itself. It is important not to let this revelation slip away, but to apply the spiritual pressure of the Holy Spirit. "Evidence of pastoral and psychotherapeutic experience shows that immense forces of inner resistance make self-knowledge very hard,"[13] yet for we who love God, even our inner turmoil works for the good. We are confident that where sin abounds, grace abounds even more.

Enough has been said about the part self-knowledge plays in the realization that we are sinners. What does it mean to grow in the knowledge that we are made in the image of God? Stop for a moment now to recall the creation account of Genesis — how was man created?

Usually a person recalls that God is "out there," who, in that one step of "Let there be . . . ," creates Adam from the earth. It is just like the creation process for the rest of creation, God is mightily transcendent, period. It may be a somewhat toned down transcendence, as when God walks with Adam in the garden, but it's a mighty transcendence nevertheless. Scripture does not emphasize this as much as we are inclined to do. Genesis says man was created differently from the rest of creation, that there was a two-step process of creation for man. First, God created a cadaver that looked like a man, and secondly he breathed his breath, his Holy Spirit, into it and it became a living human being. The one factor that makes a human being a *human* being is the life of God within. We are made in the image of God, with a freedom and a capacity to consent that is akin to God.

This explains the illusions and desires for a false-self that we have. Namely, they are founded on a half-truth. In a certain way, we are made to be "god-like." [14] God made us to be his sons and daughters. Yet we are not his equal, we have neither the omnipotence nor the absolute freedom of God. Jesus says the kingdom of God is within you *(Luke 17:21)*. St. Bernard writes,

"It does not behoove you, O man, to cross the seas, to penetrate the clouds, or to cross the Alps. No great journey is shown to you: If you wish to meet God, go as far as your own heart. 'Do not say in your heart, who will ascend into the heavens to bring Christ down, or who will descend into the abyss to bring Christ up from the dead. But what does righteousness based on faith say? The word is near you, on your lips and in your heart.' " *(Romans 10:6-8)*[15]

As we can see, the journey is inside of our hearts.

So the first step of truth, knowing the truth about ourselves, involves grasping our sinfulness and knowing that we are made in God's image; grasping both God's transcendence and his immanence. One without the other will not do, that would result in either despair or pride, and God wants humility.

This balance is important. Bernard does not slip into the depressing caricature of medieval piety that focuses on sorrow for sins alone. In one of his greatest works, a commentary on the *Song of Songs*, he writes:

"Sorrow for sin is indeed necessary, but it

should not be an endless preoccupation. You must dwell also on the glad remembrance of God's loving-kindness, otherwise sadness will harden the heart and lead it more deeply into despair. . . . You can see therefore that the order of the just man's progress is expressed in the words: 'After reflecting on my behaviour, I turn my feet to your decrees' *(Psalm 119:59)*, that is, he who has endured grief and unhappiness in following his own ways can finally say: 'In the way of your decrees lies my joy, a joy beyond all wealth.' " *(Psalm 119:14)* [16]

After we have reflected on the symptoms of our behavior and seen the root of the "disease," God wants to give us repentant hearts and free us, attracting us in a deeper way than ever before to his loving-kindness which he has already placed within our hearts.

St. Bernard writes that the second step of truth is knowing others as Jesus did. Jesus had compassion on the people when they were hungry and so he fed them *(Matthew 15:32; Mark 8:2)*. He had compassion on the crowd and so he healed their sick *(Matthew 14:14; 20:34; Mark 1:41)*. Once when Jesus saw the crowd he had compassion on them because they were like sheep without a shepherd *(Matthew 9:36; Mark 6:34)*. He had compassion on the widow of Nain and raised her son from the dead *(Luke 7:13)*.

Bernard insists that we can only have true compassion for our brothers and sisters after self-knowledge. Knowing the truth about others before knowing the truth about ourselves would result in arrogance and judgment of them: a complete lack of mercy. When we realize we are in the same position, then we will have compassion. Then we will learn to forgive seventy times seven.

The third and last step of truth is knowing God himself in purity of heart. For St. Bernard, self-knowledge involves much effort on our part while purity of heart is almost entirely the work of the Holy Spirit within us. Purity of heart does not mean, as we saw in the story of the Desert Fathers, that we no longer have evil or vain thoughts and desires. Rather, it means that we see their illusion and no longer yield or submit to them or make them the foundation of our lives. We confess our helplessness to God and rest and are comforted in him alone.

A key tool the Lord uses here is compunction, which is very different from introspection. The Lord does not want a hiding of ourselves within ourselves, but a liberation of ourselves from the inside out. Thomas Merton writes,

"In the language of medieval asceticism, the clear sighted recognition and mature acceptance of our own limitations is called 'compunction.' Compunction is a spiritual grace, an insight into our own depths which, in one glance, sees through our illusions about ourselves, sweeps aside our self-deceptions and daydreams, and shows us ourselves exactly as we are. But at the same time it is a movement of love and freedom, a liberation from falsity, a glad and grateful acceptance of the truth, with the resolution to live in contact with the deep spiritual reality which has been opened up to our vision: the reality of God's will in our own lives."[17]

This compunction is a quiet yet powerful thing. St. Bernard writes that it is a fire "which is God himself, which consumes but does not afflict." He writes of a "delightful desolation" and tells us:

"When you experience this power which totally changes you and the love which sets you on fire, understand that the Lord is present in your heart."[18]

"Happy the pure in heart: they shall see God" *(Matthew 5:8).*

We do not journey alone through this land of unlikeness . . . God has given us his Holy Spirit.

5

The Twentieth Century

There are two things in this chapter which will shed a modern light on purity of heart. First, in the Vatican Council we see the call to purity of heart as holiness being clearly extended to everyone. Second, Bernard Lonergan, S.J.'s concept of "knowledge" provides us with deeper insights into what the obstacles to knowledge are, and what knowledge of ourselves, others and God means.

Vatican Council II

As we consider the documents of Vatican II, we will see how similar is St. Bernard's understanding of the make-up of man to that of the Council Fathers, and how everyone, not only a select few, are called to the purity of heart which is holiness.

First we look at part I of Vatican II's Pastoral Constitution on the Church in the Modern World entitled "The Church and Man's Calling." Below are some excerpts[19] that show the retained image-lost likeness understanding of man's make-up.

Sacred Scripture teaches that man was created "to the image of God." (12)

Authentic freedom is an exceptional sign of the divine image within man. (17)

To the sons of Adam he (Christ) restores the divine likeness which had been disfigured from the first sin onward. (22)

The Christian man, conformed to the likeness of that Son who is the firstborn of many brothers, receives "the first fruits of the Spirit" *(Romans 8:23)* by which he becomes capable of discharging the new law of love. (22)

Wounded by sin, man experiences rebellious stirrings in his body. But the very dignity of man postulates that man glorify God in his body and forbid it to serve the evil inclinations of his heart. (14)

(Man) finds re-enforcement in this profound insight (that he has an immortal soul) whenever he enters into his own heart. God, who probes the heart, awaits him there. (14)

We see here, in the words of the Council Fathers, the same expression of the misery and dignity of man that Bernard uses. The glory of man is that he is created in the image of God, which is signified by his freedom and bestows on him a dignity sur-

passing all of creation. His problem is that his likeness to God has been disfigured or lost. Wounded
by sin, there is internal rebellion against the law of
love and so he turns love inward, creating his own
little world, a false-ego-self.

The Christian life is seen as a journey from the
land of unlikeness to the land where God's unsel-
fish love reigns in our hearts. God is aware that we
cannot journey alone, "for he sent the Holy Spirit
upon all men that he might inspire them from
within to love God . . . and that they might love
one another as Christ loved them."[20] This striving
for the perfection of charity, this aiming at the
immediate goal of purity of heart, this journey in
which we have the Holy Spirit for companion and
guide, is a journey into holiness.

All of us are to journey into holiness and purity
of heart. It is easy to picture laymen saying parish
priests are called to holiness, diocesan priests saying the religious orders are called to holiness, the
religious saying the Trappists are called to holiness,
the Trappists saying the Carthusians are called to
holiness, the Carthusians saying only God is holy.
This unholy passing of the buck is not the word of
God. "The Lord Jesus, the divine Teacher and
Model of all perfection, preached holiness of life to
each and every one of his disciples, regardless of
their situation: 'You must therefore be perfect just
as your heavenly Father is perfect (Matthew
5:48).' " [20] Again the Council Fathers say, "Thus
it is evident to everyone that all the faithful of
Christ of whatever rank or status are called to the

fullness of the Christian life and to perfection of charity."[20] The Vatican Council is the clearest statement ever that the journey into purity of heart is for each and every one of us.

The Council also concerns itself with the pathway or steps along the journey, much as Bernard spoke of asceticism as a preliminary and the three steps of truth. "Each must share frequently in the sacraments, the Eucharist especially, and in liturgi-

cal rites. Each must apply himself constantly to prayer, self-denial, active brotherly service and the exercise of all the virtues."[20] The means of purification for most of us will be different than a monk's. A monk is purified especially in prayer which is his life's work and in obedience to his abbot. Most of us would experience a passive purification in our particular life's work and in submission to circumstances.[21] As the Council puts it:

"All of Christ's faithful, therefore, whatever be the conditions, duties, and circumstances of their lives, will grow in holiness day by day through these very situations, if they accept all of them with faith from the hand of their heavenly Father, and if they cooperate with the divine will by showing every man through their earthly activities the love with which God has loved the world."[20]

Let us journey then, confident that we have been called into holiness by God. We dare not refuse. We need not fear because his grace is with us. It is with the help of his grace that we even desire to begin the journey. We can rest assured that he who initiated in us this good work will bring it to completion, giving us more than we could ever ask for or imagine.

What Is Really Knowing

At times it is easy to journey along the path into purity of heart; at other times it is hard. We encounter roadblocks, detours, obstacles. Some crossroads are not clearly marked for us, some parts of the road are even blown up and seemingly destroyed. This would be bad enough if it were a highway, but it is only a narrow path which is not easy to stay on when difficulties come either from the world, the flesh or the devil. And so we need to pray for wisdom as a guide, knowing that God will always provide for us.

It is common to read of warnings against various forms of illusions and self-delusions in devotional and ascetical writings. These are warnings against obstacles we encounter on our journey. Modern psychology gives us added insight into this from the point of view of our defense mechanisms.[11]

St. Bernard's exposition of the journey into purity of heart is in terms of the three steps of truth: knowing ourselves, knowing others and knowing God. Hence, the obstacles on the journey can be seen as obstacles to knowing. We can be more prepared for the journey of knowing ourselves, others and God if we correctly understand what "knowing" is, what is not really "knowing" though we presume it to be, and what is the bias we have that distorts "knowing." Father Lonergan has devoted his life's work to these and related areas, and we will consider them in turn.

First, what is "knowing"? Fr. Lonergan sees human knowing as a dynamic structure where our experience leads to a judgment, "yes" or "no," that our understanding is indeed correct. In his own words:

"Now human knowing involves many distinct

and irreducible activities: seeing, hearing, smelling, touching, tasting, inquiring, imagining, understanding, conceiving, reflecting, weighing the evidence, judging.

"No one of these activities, alone and by itself, may be named human knowing. An act of ocular vision may be perfect as ocular vision; yet if it occurs without any accompanying glimmer of understanding, it is mere gaping, so far from being the beau ideal of human knowing, is just stupidity. As merely seeing is not human knowing, so for the same reason merely hearing, merely smelling, merely touching, merely tasting may be parts, potential components, of human knowing, but they are not human knowing itself.

"What is true of sense, is no less true of understanding. Without the prior presentations of sense, there is nothing for a man to understand; and when there is nothing to be understood, there is no occurrence of understanding. Moreover, the combination of the operations of sense and of understanding does not suffice for human knowing. There must be added judging. To omit judgment is quite literally silly: it is only by judgment that there emerges a distinction between fact and fiction, logic and sophistry, philosophy and myth, history and legend, astronomy and astrology, chemistry and alchemy.

"Nor can one place human knowing in judging to the exclusion of experience and understanding. To pass judgment on what one does not understand is, not human knowing, but human arrogance. To pass judgment independently of all experience is to set fact aside.

"Human knowing, then, is not experience alone, not understanding alone, not judgment alone; it is not a combination of only experience and understanding, or of only experience and judgment, or of only understanding and judgment; finally, it is not something totally apart from experience, understanding and judgment. Inevitably, one has to regard an instance of human knowing, not as this or that operation, but as a whole whose parts are operations. It is a structure and, indeed, a materially dynamic structure."[22]

While this may seem both elementary and unnecessarily complex, a grasp of the structure of human knowing bears good fruit. Once a person validly knows something (i.e., has made a judgment about his understanding of experience being correct or incorrect), then he has a basis for authentic human living. Only then is it fully possible to decide to live in accordance with what we know to be true.

Second, what is not really "knowing" though we presume it to be? In light of Fr. Lonergan's conception of knowing as a dynamic structure of experience, understanding and judgment, there are various possibilities which he lists above which people might mistake for knowing. We should consider if any one of these applies to us. It would radically affect the process of knowing ourselves, others and

God, which is the journey into purity of heart.

There are those who think their knowledge is mere experience. Their motto is: "to see it is to know it." Fr. Lonergan considers such a notion "stupidity," if the person actually operates on a level of reacting to pleasurable or unpleasurable sensations without understanding and judgment. Such a person will never think of applying his knowledge of himself to areas that need changing. This person will mistake the feeling content of a religious experience for actual knowledge of God.

There are also those who think knowledge is mere understanding. They live in a world of concepts neither grounded in actual fact nor critically judged. There are those who think knowledge is mere judgment. They live at the mercy of hidden motivations and whims, which they cannot unearth so as to evaluate, modify, repent or change.

Others think knowledge is only experience and understanding. They are easily deluded since there is no critical reflection as to whether or not their understanding is correct. As soon as they achieve *an* understanding of an experience, they act on it without critically evaluating whether or not it is *the* understanding of their experience.

Some men think knowledge is only experience and judgment. Fr. Lonergan calls this human arrogance. There are those who think knowledge is only understanding and judgment. They are not living in the real world. They set fact aside and come up with theories and resolutions that never work in practice.

We need to be converted from the assumption that we know ourselves, others, or God by mere looking or feeling. This is an error common to many and in Fr. Lonergan's words:

"As soon as they begin to speak of knowing, of objectivity, of reality, there crops up the assumption that all knowing must be something like looking. To be liberated from that blunder, to discover the self-transcendence proper to the human process of coming to know, is to break off long-ingrained habits of thought and speech. It is to acquire the mastery in one's own house that is to be had only when one knows precisely what one is doing when one is knowing. It is a conversion, a new beginning, a fresh start. It opens the way to ever further clarifications and developments."[23]

Conversion to true human knowing has a relationship to moral conversion which is a change in the basis of our decisions from satisfactions to values. Our decision to live out authentically what we know to be true will be colored by self-deception if the process of our coming to know something as true is mere looking or feeling. Vice-versa, we will tend to rationalize, to change what we know to be true, if we do not decide to live according to this knowledge. Hence, the importance of correctly understanding "knowing" on our journey toward purity of heart.

This is not to be seen as human effort alone, although it does involve hard work on our part. God's grace moves us to it and we are given the gift of his love which urges us to decide to live in accordance with what we know to be true. And this in turn encourages us to reflect on what we know to be true and critically judge if it is indeed true. The important thing then, is the gift of God's love for he has first loved us. As he draws us to fall in love with him, he will lead us to the fullness of truth. An academic and philosophical understanding of epistomology is not needed here, for not everyone can attain such knowledge, yet God will provide for everyone. What is needed is courage and honesty, for as the saying goes, "where there's a will there's a way."

Third, what is the bias we have that distorts knowing? A major bias is a mistaken notion of what knowing is, which we have touched on above. The deeper issue here, however, is that to be converted to the truth we must have an insight into it that forms the core of our understanding. Although we can rest assured that God's grace will provide us with all we need, we must cooperate with it. But, "Just as insight can be desired, so too it can be unwanted. Besides the love of light, there can be a love of darkness."[24] This bias results in blindspots, a repression of the line of thinking that would lead to the unwanted insight, an inhibition of thoughts that would lead to the needed line of thinking.

The point that we need to become aware of is the self-deception that results from such a bias against insight into our oversights and the systematic elimination of them from the various areas of our life. There may be a measure of self-suspicion and disquiet, perhaps an uneasy conscience in some areas. These are signs that an area needs light shed on it, the oversight uncovered, the resultant self-deception cast out and its application to the rest of our life pursued.

To conclude, a reevaluation of the chapel incident (page 43) might prove useful. As the doors opened, and I knelt upright, I felt disquieted, embarrassed, uneasy. The first temptation was merely to experience it and go no further, to ignore, overlook, and take no notice. The next temptation was to placate my conscience and say, "I'll try not to do that next time." It is not sufficient to leave it there. I need to understand what is really wrong here; I need to arrive at the "disease," and not settle for the mere symptoms. I need to overcome my reluctance to ask the right questions.

So the question arises: "Why did I kneel upright when the doors opened?" The thought comes, "I was going to do so at that time anyway, and besides, I did not want to scandalize anyone by having him see me half-asleep in the chapel." This is *an* understanding but is it the right one? The temptation is to settle for *any* understanding and think no more of it, but true self-knowledge involves another step. I have to make a judgment as to whether or not this is the *correct* understanding. The answer is obviously "no," not because this understanding might not be correct in other circumstances, but because it does not explain my uneasiness, my embarrassment, and so I have to discard that understanding as false. I need to overcome the inclination to repress thoughts that lead to a more profound understanding.

And so the insight comes: "I want people to respect and esteem me." The temptation here again is to settle for that, to go no further. I need to reflect critically and judge, "Is that so?" and, "What does that mean?" As I confront the real reasons honestly, going through the whole process of "knowing" again to arrive at a deeper level, things begin to come out. I do not want people to respect me on the basis of who I actually am, rather I want them to view me the way I do myself with the false-self I have constructed, not according to the reality that I cannot even admit to myself.

Although I have made a decision to follow God, these unconscious motivations and hidden agenda distort my daily life. God wants to free me from them. These hidden desires are not the "real" me, yet they are a part of my heart that I must come to terms with in order that God can free me.

At this point, another temptation against self-knowledge arises: the desire to go no further, to settle for being narrowly more aware that whenever I am alone, half-asleep in a chapel I will have this hidden desire if someone comes in. To stop here is to lose almost all the fruit I could have gathered from the knowledge if I used it wisely.

A question arises here that requires much courage in order to face honestly and that, if so faced, bears much fruit. "How far has the 'disease' spread? Is every area of my life tainted with this desire for my own glory? Is this hidden desire of mine associated with other inclinations? Do they also have a subsurface distortion? Do I really want to be freed from it? What would that mean? What is this false-self I have constructed that would have to be given up? Am I willing to change my view of who I am, knowing that it means being plunged from my comfortable, settled view of myself to an as yet unexperienced something that I am unsure of? How deep has my decision to live for God really gone? Am I willing to go all the way? Am I willing to allow God to do major heart surgery?"

When I know myself to this extent, it becomes possible to engage in a more profound repentance of the root cause of my sin. With the gift of God's love, it is now possible to decide authentically to live out what I know to be true, to open my heart to God more radically.

At this point it is also possible to harden my heart to God more than ever before. The reason my subconscious rebels against this insight is because the more I know myself, the harder it is to resist basic questions that spell death for the false-self that has been constructed. The alternatives become crystal clear. If I choose life, the death warrant is signed on the hold this hidden desire has on me. The more I know myself, the more God is able to say: " . . . I set before you life or death, blessing or curse. Choose life, then, so that you and your descendants may live, in the love of Yahweh your God, obeying his voice, clinging to him; for in this your life consists, and on this depends your long stay in the land which Yahweh swore to your fathers Abraham, Isaac and Jacob he would give them" *(Deuteronomy 30:19-20).*

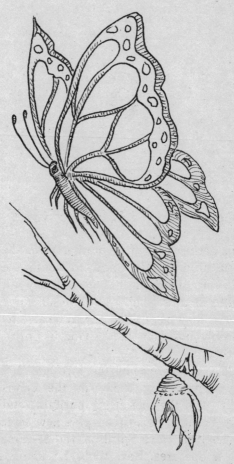

Freedom flows from letting ourselves be touched and changed.

66

6

Giving Our Hearts to God

Jesus desires to capture our hearts and become Lord of them. His Spirit, as we have seen in scripture and tradition, has been freely given as first fruits to those who call upon his name, that their hearts may be purified and so be able to enter more deeply into the love of God in Christ Jesus our Lord.

People are experiencing the love and power of God in a new way today in the charismatic renewal,[25] and the role of the purifying and healing Holy Spirit is being seen in a new light. The working of the Holy Spirit in the sacrament of Penance is one area. Rev. Michael Scanlon, in his pamphlet, *The Power of Penance*,[26] explores some of the ways in which he has been experiencing the healing of people's hearts. There are many other areas. We will now consider the progressive giving of our hearts to God in the four areas that St. Bernard wrote of: the preliminary of asceticism, growing in self-knowledge, growing in compassion for our brothers and sisters, and purity of heart in knowing God and giving ourselves to him.

Asceticism — Freedom for Knowing

The Christian life is a journey through the land of unlikeness towards the restoration of the freedom of the children of God. No one is able to make the journey by the power of the Holy Spirit alone. Everyone needs to be an active member of a Christian community, being part of a cell that, along with other cells, forms the larger local Body of Christ. This might take the form of a family or extended family, a prayer or sharing group, etc. It is through his Body that God supports us. In God's mysterious plan, it is our response to our brothers and sisters, our relationships with them, that uncover both the light and darkness within our hearts. The first provision for the journey, then, is to be a committed member of a Christian community in an active way.[27]

To commit yourself to a life together with others in the Lord demands more than mere intellectual assent. A Christian community life does not happen merely because a family or a group of people live together and are all Christians, even when they have intellectually agreed that they want to live together in Christ. It means breaking down that interior resistance and hardness of heart which is called "self-will," a determination to seek what you think is your private good in preference to the good of others. This self-will, a deep impurity of heart, is inseparable from fear, anxiety and spiritual slavery.

Life in the Body of Christ gets to the heart of man's problem. As David Knowles wrote:

> "The first and most fatal of all sins was a sin of pride issuing in disobedience, and it is common experience that pride, the quasi-natural unwillingness to submit to control, is the basic spiritual fault."[28]

God has called us to a high vocation and given us the gift of community life in him, whatever the concrete form of our "cell," because that is what will deeply satisfy us. Living in an environment of love and care for one another in the power of the Holy Spirit is why we are made, it is the normal means God has given for a deep peace and joy and all the fruits of the Holy Spirit.

Part of the reason God has formed, and is renewing, Christian community on every level is because it so effectively breaks in upon the privacy and exclusiveness of our self-will that leads us to the illusion of a false-ego-self. It is expressly designed to purify us and break down the resistance which prevents us from giving our hearts to God without reservation. It is never intended to encroach on one's personality nor to deprive one of true freedom, yet when lived in the power of the Spirit, it gradually strips away the false-self and undermines false ideas of freedom.

To live in Christian community in the power of the Holy Spirit, much more is needed than sacrifice and involvement. A radical commitment of our hearts is necessary to follow Christ and to live in his Body. Jesus said:

> "If any man comes to me without hating his father, mother, wife, children, brothers, sisters, yes and his own life too, he cannot be my disciple." *(Luke 14:26)*

Jesus is asking not for "hate," but for total detachment, renouncing all we hold dear so that we can cling fully to him.

When a person begins to experience this kind of demand from the Lord, in the Body of Christ, there is often an internal resistance. Experiences in prayer are one thing, but when the Lord says to us, "Submit to the discipline, order and headship[29] in the community; submit to listening patiently to the brother or sister who annoys you; submit to doing things the way your brothers prefer and not the way you like," our response is, "But what about my freedom? Can't I be free?" Feelings inside of us tense up and we feel restricted, shut in, confined. Freedom is seen as being able to do whatever I want to do whenever I want to do it. This false idea of freedom tells us to keep all the options open. Yet this very attitude is what keeps a person from becoming free. He finds himself preoccupied with making trivial decisions because he does not want to make the really major decision that will close off the options. This person cannot be singlehearted because he wants to guard options for himself, always worrying that he might lose his life.

Jesus says: " . . . anyone who loses his life for my sake will find it" *(Matthew 16:25)*. He wants us to close off certain options, to follow the narrow path and to experience the freedom of his Holy Spirit. Jesus wants us to have deep internal freedom, a freedom to love, a freedom to be faithful, a freedom to be joyful. When a person tries to keep all the options open he binds himself so that he cannot be touched. Real freedom comes from letting ourselves be deeply touched by God himself, and by our brothers and sisters. Freedom flows from letting ourselves be touched and changed, a freedom from fear, isolation and anxiety. The healing of our hearts that the Lord wants to accomplish through his body is the ongoing process of true freedom growing. Jesus is the Lord of his body and so we can have confidence that our hearts will be healed more and more for where sin abounds, grace abounds more abundantly.

Asceticism, present on all levels of Christian community, grates against false ideas of freedom. By the power of the Holy Spirit it can be a preliminary that leads us into purity of heart, the freedom of the children of God.

My household, the group of Christians with whom I live, prayerfully considered one day what the Lord wanted in the area of conversation at the dinner table. We reflected on what the Lord was saying. We came across a number of scriptural passages that urged us to speak in a way that builds up. We decided to try something new. At the dinner table, we would think before speaking, and consider whether what we were about to say was something that would build up the brothers. If it would not, then we would be silent. At dinner the following day, there was an unusual amount of silence! It takes time to learn how to build up one another in the right ways. Not uttering things that will be unedifying is asceticism, just as fasting from food or sleep would be. The immediate internal reaction could easily be: "But what about my freedom to say whatever I want?" Jesus wants to bless us with a different attitude, one that will enable us to grow into the freedom to love.

From this example a number of points can be made. First, asceticism should be something very normal and tailored to the kind of life we live. Second, it is an opportunity to maintain a balanced perspective. For example: it insures that speaking our own mind does not begin to have a priority of importance over building up the brothers. Third, asceticism is a preliminary, not an end in itself. It is valuable only insofar as it reflects an internal reality. To agree to speak only in an edifying way (as opposed to engaging in trivial topics such as the weather) and then merely to externalize the resolution is valueless, even harmful. Such a practice forces you to live according to the law. It is usually communicated non-verbally to everyone anyway.

Fourth, since it is not an end in itself, asceticism

must be directed towards its proper end. We need God's wisdom to see which things will help us to attain this end, and which will only complicate matters. If the end is to build up one another, some means to achieve this might create just the opposite. For instance, if we had decided that just one person would speak during the entire meal, it would not have been too upbuilding. For some people, in other circumstances, deciding the same thing might not be wise. Similarly, what we decided to do might not be wise for us a few months later.

There are hundreds of other examples of asceticism to give in every area of our lives: the way we relate to our spouses, family, members of our community, the boss at work, headship, scheduled prayers, the degree of privacy, paying attention to other people when they speak, etc. The Lord wants to give us wisdom to know his will in our situation. "If there is anyone of you who needs wisdom, he must ask God, who gives to all freely and ungrudgingly; it will be given to him" *(James 1:5)*.

In concluding the topic of asceticism, let us recall the main point: we need the right kind of asceticism in our life if we are to persevere in the journey. It is hard to say which is worse, no asceticism or wrong asceticism. The point is not to attempt great feats of discipline, but to grow in purity of heart. See to what kind of asceticism wisdom leads us, discover why we are doing it (remember, achieving knowledge is hard work), and evaluate it regularly.

Asceticism is a needed preliminary, yet if that is the focus, then life is lived according to the law. We have been called to live according to the Spirit, to live in the truth in the light of God's love. God's Spirit leads us to live in his own love. St. Bernard's first step of truth that leads to the purity of heart, which is God's love, is self-knowledge or humility.

Knowing ourselves, in reality, means having a healthy balance between our awareness of our weakness and our awareness of God's personal love for us. Often a major obstacle to true humility is low self-esteem or a poor self-image.

I recall a young man taking a series of seminars on the Christian life given in our community. He was in my discussion group. Frequently he would speak of his past failings, belittling himself. Our encouragement seemed wasted. One day after the seminar he came to talk to me about his uselessness. He said he wanted to leave the seminars to which he was committed since everything would proceed well without him. He said no one would miss him since there was nothing he could contribute to people. He felt he was worthless and lived under a spirit of condemnation. His poor self-image blocked his growth with God as well as people. We should not mistake this for the virtue of humility. His was an emotional problem. He was not in touch with the truth of his being the crown of creation, the image of God, a person the Lord loves. Jesus came to save us from this, to make

God's love for us perfectly clear.

This obstacle of low self-esteem occurs quite frequently and people need to come to grips with it. It manifests itself in many ways, especially in community life, with our families or those with whom we live, and deep relationships with others. In the young man above it surfaced in a sense of uselessness that made him want to give up or not attempt any task or relationship.

God wants to heal what is wrong in the basic way we view ourselves. This "disease" is the source of all the symptoms; it is the ninety percent of the iceberg that is below the surface of the water. This unhealthy view of ourselves easily links together two contradictory beliefs. On the one hand we feel inadequate, have a poor self-image, due to being very aware of our weakness and sin. On the other hand we compensate for it by constructing a false-ego-self with delusions of grandeur, imagining that we should be relatively omnipotent. This happens in as many ways as there are people; each way, as each person, is unique.

We are not innocent at all because we are trying to save ourselves in a disastrous way by constructing a false-ego-self instead of accepting God's salvation by means of his love in Jesus. As we come to a deep awareness of what our problem is, and repent of it, God will save us. Repentance and conversion, ongoing for our whole lives, is the opposite side of the coin of falling in love with God.

Having a good self-image is a gift Jesus wants to give to all. It is not pride, but rather, humility. God calls us to love our neighbor as ourselves. This love for ourselves is not meant to be egotistical and based on a need to compensate for a poor self-image, but a deep respect, acceptance and confidence in the basic goodness the Lord has placed there. God does not make trash and he has made us. A good self-image involves integrity — be honest with yourself first of all. Be yourself, not a hypocrite living behind a facade, a mask, a role, a false-ego-self. Seek out the vocation to which God is calling you and be faithful to it. Authentically live out what you know to be true. Look at the people God sends into your life and relate to them. If you cannot meet a person's gaze when you talk to him, find out why and ask God to heal it.[30] If you cannot be comfortable in a relationship, find out why and ask God to heal that, too. Jesus wants to give abundant life. If you have an overwhelming sense of guilt, find out why and ask God to heal it. God will give us the wisdom and power we need *(James 1:2-15)* to know the truth, to repent, to receive wholeness. God wants to heal and deliver us. Seek it.

Jesus wants us to have a healthy attitude towards self. In God's plan we can enjoy ourselves and deeply accept ourselves in the light of his love. As we experience God's total acceptance of ourselves, we feel grateful.

After I came in touch with the sin within my heart, when I knelt upright as the chapel doors opened, I experienced God's total acceptance of me and it led to gratitude. As I described earlier (page 61) I felt distressed and embarrassed at first. Then, with the help of grace, I was able to ask the right questions and enter into the line of thinking that led to knowing the source, the root sin, the "disease" — I wanted people to respect and esteem me in a sinful way. I accepted the fact that it was part of my heart.

I also came into touch with a deep desire to follow God. It was not a mere stoic decision to follow God, although I had committed my life to him and decided to follow him wherever he led me. I experienced a deep attraction to him, a desire to be pure for him, to be cleansed of hidden motivations, to live for him and no longer for myself. I wept at the thought that God had given his life for me, yet I was repaying him like this. I began to experience a burning love for God in the depths of my heart which I sensed was cleansing me painfully from the hold of this desire for undue esteem. I began to experience a freedom and a liberation from that kind of self-deception. It no longer had the same power over me.

I knew that the love of God which was welling up in my heart was a gift from him. At the same time, I was so much in touch with my impurity and sinfulness that I could not understand why God was giving me this gift. I knew in my heart that I did not deserve this — an uncommon experience in my heart of what I doctrinally believe is true. I began to be overwhelmed with gratitude for God's goodness and love in the midst of my sinfulness. I began to rejoice in him, feeling grateful and happy.

We are called to live in God's love, to experience gratitude to God, to rejoice in him and all of his gifts, and to love him with our whole heart. We are grateful for gifts, not for things which we feel we deserve. Suppose it is your birthday. If you expect to receive a birthday present from your brother, then when you do receive it, it does not make you feel very grateful and happy. You experience an almost sterile satisfaction, a kind of negative state of not feeling cheated, of just getting what you deserve. If, however, you receive an unexpected birthday gift from someone, then you feel grateful and pleasantly surprised by this person's expression of love. You also feel a joy, a rejoicing happiness, for when we are truly grateful, then we are happy.

Knowing ourselves is seeing our sinfulness in the light of God's love. It involves a healthy attitude towards self, a good self-image. True humility involves the awareness that we depend on God's strength in our weakness. We have confidence in the fact that we are his sons and daughters. Our security, the foundation of our life, is in God. If circumstances are not ideal, that is all right, for our hope is not in ideal circumstances. If we see people fail in their love for God or their love for us, we may be saddened, but that, too, is all right, for our hope is not in the perfection of those we are close to or admire. If we see ourselves sin or fail in love, again we are saddened, but ultimately that too is all right, for our hope is not in our strength. Our hope is in the Lord our God, in him alone.

True humility is having the courage to look deeply within ourselves, yet not being trapped there, not focusing on ourselves, but looking to Jesus. It is repentance, being sorry for our sins, falling more deeply in love with God; yet not being sorry for ourselves, not wallowing in self-pity or depression, not yielding to the spirit of condemnation. It is having confidence in God, in his personal plan for our lives, in what he has shown us; yet it is neither arrogant, absolute nor naive about obstacles and our own weakness.

Humility is courage to face fundamental questions about ourselves and to be faithful to the answers God gives, hoping in him, trusting in his love.

" . . . we too, then, should throw off everything that hinders us, especially the sin that clings so easily, and keep running steadily in the race we have started. Let us not lose sight of Jesus, who leads us in our faith and brings it to perfection: for the sake of the joy which was still in the future, he endured the cross, disregarding the shamefulness of it, and from now on has taken his place at the right of God's throne. Think of the way he stood such opposition from sinners and then you will not give up for want of courage." *(Hebrews 12:1-3)*

Knowing Others — Personal Relationships

St. Bernard's second step of truth is knowing others, which is done in compassion. Knowing others before knowing ourselves leads to condemning them, to becoming angry with them. When we first know ourselves, and *then* know others, we are led to mercy.

St. Bernard, in his commentary on the *Song of Songs*, draws out what happens as we try to know and help others if we have not been filled with God's love in the process of coming to know ourselves: " . . . you rashly proceed to pour out your unfulfilled self upon others."[31] In giving others our emptiness, we are often "lacking right intention and inspired by self-conceit."[31] Those who are involved in the "charity" of helping others remove the specks in their eyes, ignorant of the planks in their own, "are more ready to speak than to listen, impatient to teach what they have not grasped, and full of presumption to govern others while they know not how to govern themselves."[31] Such a person's charity is:

"So unsound that, contrary to the commandment, it bows to flattery, flinches under fear, is upset by sadness, shrivelled by avarice, entangled by ambition, disquieted by suspicions, tormented by insults, exhausted by anxieties, puffed up by honors, consumed by envy. If you discover this chaos in your own interior, what madness drives you to insinuate yourself into other people's business? . . . For if you are mean to yourself, to whom will you be good?"[31]

This is why knowing others before knowing ourselves leads to condemning them and getting frustrated and annoyed with them. We become "cynical mask strippers."[32]

A poster I once saw said: "A Christian is one beggar telling another beggar where to find bread." Just because we know where the bread is, does not mean we are no longer beggars. We are no better than the other person, we have merely found out where the bread is that can keep us alive.

When we first know ourselves and then know others, we are led to mercy. Knowing ourselves helps us to grow in sensitivity and compassion for others. An example from conversation at the supper table will illustrate this.

Consider the common situation of a small group of people having supper together. Imagine yourself pouring out your heart to a second person there, sharing who you are and what is of value to you. As you share these intimate thoughts and feelings with him, you feel closer. At a sensitive moment you pause, about to share something with your friend which you have never shared with others, and you look up. You suddenly become aware that he has not been listening, and he has used this pause to begin a conversation with a third person at the table. You feel hurt, embarrassed and lonely.

It would be easy, at this point, to begin condemning the person, getting frustrated and angry with him, withdrawing your heart and desiring to teach him a lesson. However, if you really know yourself, you will respond differently to your hurt and embarrassment. You are aware that you have acted just like that second person quite often. You can begin to understand how preoccupying his own needs are to him, and the burdens and emptiness which prevents him from responding to you. You begin to be aware that sharing your heart in this manner is not something the person can respond to at this moment, he needs to be unburdened, to be listened to, to be loved in a different way. Instead of a bitterness that he alone is not loving, your hurt and loneliness is formed into a sorrow that we together are so far from loving one another as Jesus does. You experience a compassion for both of you together, and there is a new bond in your relationship with him. You know that you are together in being beggars, begging Jesus for unity, wholeness and love that the Lord alone can bring to fullness.

More than compassion, you grow in sensitivity in personal relationships. When a person is speaking to you, and the situation is reversed, you are more sensitive. You know both the hurt he will feel if you withhold your heart, and also the closeness and love that will grow if you give your heart. You are more sensitive when you are in the position of the third person, too. As someone is being ignored by the one speaking to you, you can refer back to what he was saying, bring him in, assure him that he is neither ignored nor unimportant. You can ease his hurt and embarrassment. God teaches how to love in compassion, to comfort.

In any personal relationship, especially a life together with others, it is important to communicate that we understand the feelings of the other person. It is not always important that we "be in his shoes"; but it is important that we understand what the shoes are that he is in, what it feels like and that we communicate this to him. Someone heard this once and said he felt this way about Pope John. He was never aware of the Holy Father's weaknesses or sins, but he felt close to him because somehow he was assured that Pope John understood where he was and what it was like. This is the kind of "knowing others" that St. Bernard is talking about.

As we relate to people we need to understand their feelings and burdens, and communicate that understanding to them. Our brothers and sisters need the power of God's love and the experience of our understanding. Gradually, with the help of the Holy Spirit, we become a source of life by reflecting the love and understanding and compassion of Jesus.

Knowing God — Prayer

At the heart of our life with God is turning to him, seeking him, being radically open to him, falling in love with him. "Seek Yahweh while he is still to be found, call to him while he is still near" *(Isaiah 55:6)*. We need to seek his will with all our hearts, not asking him to "rubber stamp" our plans. "Rubber stamping" is telling God what we want to do and merely checking with him to see if it is all right. Instead, he calls us to abandon ourselves to him. Abandonment is asking God before we have decided: "Lord, what is it you would have of me?"

God is calling us to know and experience him in a more profound way, to be faithful to him in daily prayer. Jesus wants to give the power of his Spirit in prayer, drawing us to seek him fervently and give our hearts to him in a deeper way. We know that we can come to prayer and withhold our hearts, merely be there and routinely pray. It is similar to the experience of only half-listening to a person — we are also half daydreaming or thinking of what to say next. And when the person asks our opinion, we ask him to repeat his question. When we pray we can merely be present bodily, or we can pray in our hearts. We can give our hearts to seeking God and praising him, and receive the new word the Lord has for us this very day. We can allow him to enlarge our hearts. We need to commit ourselves to a daily prayer period.[33]

Rarely does a person have a problem with prayer; it is really a problem of love, of praying just for what is gotten out of it (good feelings, feeling justified), instead of praying because we love God, want to be with him, and desire to praise him. We have to decide to live totally for God before prayer makes sense. God is calling us to fall in love with him, with our whole heart, mind, soul and strength. It is God's love flooding our hearts through the Holy Spirit that has been given to us. It grounds the conviction of St. Paul that " . . . neither death nor life, no angel, no prince, nothing that exists, nothing still to come, not any power, or height or depth, nor any created thing,

can ever come between us and the love of God
made visible in Christ Jesus our Lord" *(Romans
8:38-39)*. It is being in love without limits or
boundaries. It brings the deep set joy that remains
despite difficulties. It brings the radical peace that
the world cannot give. It bears fruit in the love for
one another that is ushering in the kingdom of
God. Being in love with God is what our life with
him is all about. Falling in love with God is his gift
to us that makes us desire to be empty so he can
fill us. " . . . the spirit which he sent to live in us
wants us for himself alone" *(James 4:5)*.

It is a source of life for us that before and after
our common assemblies we go into the closet, shut
the door, and commune with our Father. He
desires to give us the gift of purity of heart daily as
we enter into his presence, so that we might be in
his presence with our whole heart, and allow him
to reclaim us, and to deepen and purify our love
for him. As we confess our helplessness to God,
having only him as the foundation of our lives, we
rest and are comforted in him alone.

Jesus wants to draw us into the love of his
Father by having us drink of the Spirit. He gives us
his own Spirit to eat and drink in his Body and
Blood. St. Ephraim paraphrased the institution of
the Eucharist:

"(Jesus) called the loaf his living Body and
filled it with himself and with the Spirit. . . .
Take it and eat it in faith, never doubting that it
is my body, and that whoever eats it in faith is
eating fire and the Spirit . . . eat of it, all of you,

85

and eat the Spirit in it, for it is truly my Body."[34]

The test of our commitment is in saying, "Come, Lord Jesus, come and rule in my heart," in wanting the fire of Pentecost to be cast on the earth, in wanting fire and the Spirit to be cast into our hearts. We know that to be purified will hurt. To be faithful in prayer, in relationships, in the duties of our state of life is not easy. But God has shown us himself in his Son, Jesus; he has poured out his Holy Spirit into our hearts, and we know that nothing, nothing at all, is more important than returning to him. We want to will only our Father's will, to really be able to say, "your will be done," knowing and gladly acknowledging that we are signing our own death warrant. We want to empty ourselves into the mystery of the passion and cross, to espouse the cross in our weakness and poverty, to love the cross and to boast in Jesus. We pray: "Come Holy Spirit, come and purify our hearts. We desire to be purified. We want to die so we can live in you and you can live in us. We want to be faithful, to return to covenant faithfulness, for in faithfulness we will know you."

7

Conclusion

Many people are shocked when they first experience sin within their hearts. Combating evil situations and spiritual enemies seems easy compared to the fifth column within. As difficult as it is, yet is is deeply knowing the sin within our hearts that forms the contrite and broken heart that God will not scorn. It is this broken spirit that allows God's Holy Spirit to purify our hearts, and draw us into his love. In the *Imitation of Christ* we read:

> "That person is truly happy who has grace to avoid all things that hinder him from beholding his own sin; he is truly happy who can turn himself to God by inward compunction."[35]

There is the freedom of God's love in this truth.

No longer trying to earn our salvation, we rely on God's power in our weakness. "We are only the earthenware jars that hold this treasure, to make it clear that such an overwhelming power comes from God and not from us" *(2 Corinthians 4:7).* We no longer try to make all our weaknesses into

strengths, rather we simply open up our weaknesses so that the power of God can be made manifest through them.

The freedom of the Spirit is released as we rely on God's power in our weakness instead of our strengths. It is God's love flooding our hearts through the Holy Spirit that has been given to us. Sacrifices are no longer begrudged, for we have fallen in love with God. In his love, God pierces our hearts so that all fears are drained out. And so it is with gratefulness and joy that we enter anew into the life of God.

The journey through the land of unlikeness is not an easy one, but his Spirit guides us and great rewards come as we persevere in the journey. To seek God is to leave this world although we remain in it. Above everything, this means first of all to leave ourselves and begin to live for others. We live no longer for ourselves, but for him. Jesus calls us to follow him in being obedient unto death. To experience the life of Jesus, we must relinquish our stubborn will to live and exist as self-assertive and self-seeking individuals. To renounce the pleasure of our dearest illusions about ourselves is to die more effectively than we could ever do by martyrdom. Even if our families or brothers and sisters in a community seek to spare us our illusions, God, in his jealous love, will not spare us if we are truly seeking him. For when illusions of the false-self die, they give place to the reality of God's love which purifies our hearts and makes us a new creation.

What is needed is a final and radical renunciation of the unconscious struggle to resist the desires of others, the desire to assert ourselves against their wills, the rebellion against any controls on us, the super-sensitivity to any limitations on our independence, the desire to impose ourselves as distinct and superior, the worry and agitation that comes from striving to hide our limitations from ourselves and disguise our faults, even our emotional problems, as virtues. This final and radical renunciation is the beginning of purity of heart.

God's solution to our impurity of heart is the purifying force of the Holy Spirit working both in prayer and in daily community life. It is the sacrament of the cross. The inner pride and insecurity of fallen man must be crucified on the cross of truth. We will be made poor — emptied of the false-self we have erected, our own light which is darkness to Jesus, and our illusions that blind us to God's love. Day in and day out, submitting ourselves to one another, and in a special way to those who are over us in the Lord, is the sacrament of the cross. God purifies us and leads us into freedom and reality, delivers us from fears, strengthens us in his love, and enables us to live as his sons and daughters.

The Body of Christ in which we have been placed is a place to love and dwell, to be purified and to be prepared for the kingdom of God. There is certainly much to learn: to be faithful to brothers and sisters; to be one as Jesus and the Father are; to forgive others their faults; to submit to one another; to enter into the love and care God would have us have for one another; to grow in purity of heart which alone allows us to see God. We also must learn to love and respect our own person for the sake of God. Obviously all is not perfect in the Body of Christ. Yet we are working out our salvation here in fear and trembling and being prepared for eternal life in the Trinity.

Purity of heart is the beginning of integration within ourselves. Being freed from the necessity to serve our own unyielding, relentless and inflexible will, we begin to know the freedom and love of God's will. We see ourselves and others as we truly are in the light of the love and compassion of Jesus. No longer bound to serve our own appetites first, we find that all things bring us joy and happiness because we experience in them the glorious freedom of the sons and daughters of God: owning everything because we have nothing; having our fears cast out by perfect love; having our frustrations diminish by accepting our limitations as creatures; living in the peace and joy that comes from falling in love with God; being exuberantly happy and grateful because once we were lost and now we are found, and God did not owe it to us; counting our own light as darkness because of the value of knowing the light of Christ Jesus our Lord; rejoicing in glorious freedom because we know the truth and the truth has set us free!

Notes

1. *Jerusalem Bible,* footnote 1 of John 9:39, p. 169.
2. *Jerusalem Bible,* footnote e of Psalm 11:7, p. 795.
3. See books such as *Theological Dictionary of the New Testament,* ed. by Kittel, Eerdmans, Mich., 1965, Vol. III, p. 605 (article on Heart by Behm); and Xavier Leon-Du Four, S.J., General Editor, *Dictionary of Biblical Theology,* p. 200ff (Heart) and p. 421ff. (Pure.)
4. Merton, Thomas, *The Wisdom of the Desert,* New Directions, N.Y., N.Y., 1970 #L.
5. See 4, #LVI.
6. Raasch, J., "The Monastic Concept of Purity of Heart and Its Sources," *Studia Monastica,* Vol. II, 1969, Fasc. 2, p. 271. This is the fourth in a series of five articles.
7. This touches upon a reality which centers around the nature of divine grace and human freedom. For a theological light on this, see Karl Rahner's article, "The Theological Concept of Concupiscentia" in *Theological Investigations,* Vol. I, Helicon Press, Baltimore, 1961, p. 347-382. Also see the many writings on the Fathers and theologians on the nature of grace and freedom.
8. Paraphrased from *The Nicene and Post-Nicene Fathers,* Second Series, Vol. XI, Erdmans, 1964, John Cassian, Conferences, p. 295ff.
9. Tunink, O.S.B., Wilfred, *Vision of Peace, A Study of Benedictine Monastic Life,* Farrar, Straus & Co., N.Y., N.Y., 1963, p. 5.
10. E. Gilson's book *(The Mystical Theology of St. Bernard,* Sheed & Ward, N.Y., N.Y., 1940) has been a valuable source for this chapter, also many of Thomas Merton's books *(The Silent Life, Seeds of Contemplation, New Seeds of Contemplation, No Man Is an Island, Seasons of Celebration, Contemplative Prayer)* and John J. Higgins' book, *Merton's Theology of Prayer.*
11. See the excellent study of defense mechanisms in this context by Arnold Uleyn, *Is It I, Lord? Pastoral Psychology and the Recognition of Guilt,* Holt, Rinehart, & Winston, N.Y., N.Y. 1969.
12. Bernard of Clairvaux, "The Steps of Humility," *Treatise II,* trans. by M. Basil Pennington, o.c.s.o., Cistercian Publications, Spencer, Mass., 1974.
13. See 11, p. 68.
14. The following is an interesting story about this by Richard Wurmbrand in *Tortured for Christ,* Diane Books, 1967, p. 44f.:

    In the prison of Gherla, a Christian named Grecu was sen-

tenced to be beaten to death. The process lasted a few weeks. He was beaten very slowly. He would be hit once on the bottom of his feet with a rubber club, and then left. After some minutes he was hit again, then a pause, then hit again. He was beaten on the testicles. Then a doctor gave him an injection. He recovered and was given very good food to restore his strength, and then he was beaten again until he died under this slow repeated beating. One who led this torture was named Reck, a member of the Central Committee of the Communist Party.

At a certain moment, Reck would say something which the Communists would often say to Christians, "You know, I am God. I have power of life and death over you. The one in heaven cannot decide to keep you in life. Everything depends on me. If I wish, you live. If I wish, you are killed. I am God!" So he mocked the Christian.

Brother Grecu, in this horrible situation, gave Reck a very interesting answer which I heard afterward from Reck himself. He said, "You don't know what a deep thing you have said. You are really a god. Every caterpillar is in reality a butterfly, if it develops rightly. You have not been created to be a torturer, a man who kills. You have been created to become a godlike being. Jesus said to the Jews of His time, 'Ye are gods.' The life of God-head is in your heart. Many who have been like you, many persecutors, as the Apostle Paul, have discovered at a certain moment, that it is shameful for a man to commit atrocities, that they can do much better things. So they have become partakers of the divine nature. Believe me, Mr. Reck, your real calling is to be a god, godlike; not a torturer."

15. Quoted in Thomas Merton's *Seasons of Celebration,* Farrar, Straus and Giroux, N.Y., N.Y., 1965, pp. 69-70.

16. Bernard of Clairvaux, *On the Song of Songs I,* Sermon 11.2, Trans. Kilian Walsh, o.c.s.o., Cistercian Publications, Spencer, Mass., 1971, p. 70.

17. Merton, Thomas, *The Silent Life,* Farrar, Straus & Cudahy, N.Y., N.Y., 1957, pp. 111-112.

18. See 17, p. 112. This is Merton's translation of sermon 57.7 of Bernard's commentary on the *Song of Songs.*

19. Text used is Abbott's *The Documents of Vatican II,* Guild, America and Association Presses, 1966. The numbers next to the quotes are the paragraphs of the document.

20. See 19. This and following quotations are taken from the Dogmatic Constitution on the Church, sections 39-42.

21. Cf. Cuskelly, E.J., *A Heart to Know Thee,* Paulist Press, N.Y., N.Y., 1963, pp. 162-166 on "The Apostolate" which deals with passive purification for noncontemplatives.

22. Lonergan, B., *Collection,* ed. by F.E. Crowe, Herder and Herder, N.Y., N.Y., 1967, pp. 222-223.

23. _____ , *Method in Theology,* Herder and Herder, N.Y., N.Y., 1972, pp. 239-240.

24. _____ , *Insight, A Study of Human Understanding,* Longmans, N.Y., N.Y., 1957, p. 191.

25. The Pentecostal movement, or the charismatic renewal, is the fastest growing movement in the Church today. It is a movement of spiritual renewal in faith and people touched by it often form prayer groups where they gather together for shared prayer. The story of the beginnings of the movement are well documented in the following books: *The Pentecostal Movement in the Catholic Church,* Rev. Edward O'Connor, C.S.C., 1971; *Catholic Pentecostals,* Kevin and Dorothy Ranaghan, 1969; *As the Spirit Leads Us,* edited by the Ranaghans, 1971. These books and others on the charismatic renewal are available from the Communications Center, Drawer A, Notre Dame, Ind. 46556.

26. Scanlon, T.O.R., Rev. Michael, *The Power of Penance,* Ave Maria Press, 1973.

27. There are many forms of Christian communities, the most common being parishes and religious orders. Families are meant to be "cells" within a parish. Unfortunately, however, a person often is not able to find the fellowship, expectant faith and community life in a way that can actively support him in that "cell" alone. Most areas have prayer groups where this kind of fellowship is more possible. There is likely a prayer group not far from where you are. You can obtain a directory of their locations and people to contact by writing to the Communications Center, address in note 25.

28. Knowles, David, *From Pachomius to St. Ignatius,* Clarendon Press, Oxford, 1966, p. 70.

29. Headship and submission is something that needs to be part of every Christian life. It happens in a variety of ways, does not always mean the same thing and is being renewed today.

Heads are those who are "over you in the Lord," who are pastorally responsible for you and serve you in a particular way, and to whom you submit. Examples are on a variety of levels. A husband is head of his wife. A father is head of his family. A pastor is head of those in his parish. A religious superior is head of the members of the order in his house. A bishop is head of those in his diocese. A spiritual director is head of the one he directs. A parish council or a parish society president is head of the council or society. A prayer group leader is head of the members of the prayer group, etc.

These are not all the same kind of headship. We should not level off or equate all of them. Some are formal and depend on ordination. Some are binding and depend on a vow of obedience. Some are natural and depend on family units. Some are informal and depend on the group that gathers together. Most are a mixture.

Headship and submission do not always mean the same thing. It might mean an obediential submission. More commonly it means a consultative submission where you share with your head what you believe the Lord is saying, why you believe the Lord is saying that, and together come to a unity. Headship is a gift from God and its purpose is to draw a body into unity, to give overall direction and guidance.

A problem today that headship and submission are mostly in theory and not in practice. Often people, especially religious, after a bad experience, have gone to the other extreme of not headship but mere administration – having a "facilitator" instead of a head. Yet if the authority of headship to bring about unity is undermined, then the Christian community is undermined. The solution to *bad* headship, is *good* headship, not *no* headship. Headship and submission does not conflict with collegiality or subsidiarity. Any group that is to come together in unity in Christ has to come to grips with this area.

People in the charismatic renewal are rediscovering this gift, especially those who have been led to form a more stable community life. It does, however, apply to all. For an application of its role in marriage and family life, see *The Christian Family*, by Larry Christenson, Bethany Fellowship, Minneapolis, Minn., 1970.

30. Fr. Michael Scanlon has written a book that will aid one in having a feeling for this: *Inner Healing*, Paulist Press, N.Y., N.Y., 1974. Another valuable book is *Healing* by Fr. Francis MacNutt, O.P., Ave Maria Press, Notre Dame, Ind., 1974.

31. See 16, pp. 134-135. This and following quotations are from sermon 18.2-18.4.

32. See Uleyn's comments on this (note 11), p. 89ff.

33. For help in starting a daily prayer period and entering into it the right way, see Ralph Martin's *Hungry for God*, Doubleday, N.Y., N.Y., 1974; Paul Sauve's *Petals of Prayer*, Living Flame Press, Locust Valley, N.Y., 1974; and *The Art of Prayer, An Orthodox Anthology*, compiled by Igumen Chariton of Valamo, trans. by E. Kadlovbousky and E.M. Palmer, Faber, London, 1966.

34. Quoted in "The Holy Spirit in the Eucharist," Boris Bobrinskoy, *Christian* magazine (Institute of Christian Studies, 7 Margaret St., London, W. 1) Vol. 2, No. 1, Whitsun, 1974, p. 25.

35. a Kempis, Thomas, *The Imitation of Christ*, Doubleday Image book, Garden City, N.Y., trans. by Harold Gardiner, p. 59.

About the Author

Joseph Breault received an M.S. in physics from Stevens Institute of Technology. Turning down fellowship offers for a Ph.D., he decided to give his life to full-time Christian service. He is one of the "shepherds," or overall leaders, of Ignatius House Community, a Catholic Charismatic Community in Rutherford, New Jersey. Its hundred or so members believe God has called them to a vocation of love and unity in a common life together of prayer, sharing in household, financial responsibility, service and submission to headship. Their apostolate includes outreach in charismatic renewal conferences, retreats, evangelism and a diocesan renewal center. He is presently the head of a household with nine other men, some of whom are also committed to celibacy.

Since 1971, Joe has taught one or two courses as a member of the part-time faculty in the Math/Physics Department of Fairleigh Dickinson University in Rutherford. He is a member of the North American Advisory Committee of the Catholic Charismatic Renewal and Chairman of the Eastern Service Committee of the Catholic Charismatic Renewal. In the latter capacity, he has responsibility for the Eastern General Conferences of the Catholic Charismatic Renewal which have been held in Atlantic City.